Different Tails of Animals

by Grace Hansen

abdobooks.com

Published by Abdo Kids, a division of ABDO, P.O. Box 398166, Minneapolis, Minnesota 55439.
Copyright © 2024 by Abdo Consulting Group, Inc. International copyrights reserved in all countries.
No part of this book may be reproduced in any form without written permission from the publisher.
Abdo Kids Jumbo™ is a trademark and logo of Abdo Kids.

Printed in the United States of America, North Mankato, Minnesota.

052023

092023

THIS BOOK CONTAINS
RECYCLED MATERIALS

Photo Credits: BluePlanetArchive.com, Getty Images, Shutterstock

Production Contributors: Teddy Borth, Jennie Forsberg, Grace Hansen
Design Contributors: Candice Keimig, Pakou Moua

Library of Congress Control Number: 2022946800
Publisher's Cataloging-in-Publication Data

Names: Hansen, Grace, author.

Title: Different tails of animals / by Grace Hansen

Description: Minneapolis, Minnesota : Abdo Kids, 2024 | Series: Amazing animal features | Includes online
    resources and index.

Identifiers: ISBN 9781098266288 (lib. bdg.) | ISBN 9781098266981 (ebook) | ISBN 9781098267339
    (Read-to-me ebook)

Subjects: LCSH: Animals--Juvenile literature. | Body composition--Juvenile literature. | Tail--Juvenile
    literature. | Zoology--Juvenile literature.

Classification: DDC 591.1--dc23

Table of Contents

Different Tails of Animals

There are many different tails in the animal kingdom. Tails help animals survive in different ways!

Balance

Many land animals have **evolved** to have tails. The main reason for having a tail is to help with balance.

Cats have long, thin tails that

help them move over certain

surfaces. Tails also help cats

balance as they move quickly

or leap at **prey**.

Movement

Fish and **marine** mammals have tails that move them through water. Fish tails move from side to side. They come in many different shapes.

A **marine** mammal's tail is long and flat. The tail moves up and down. This motion brings the animal to the water's surface to breathe.

Defense

Some animal tails are used as defense. Rattlesnakes give a warning by making a loud noise with their tails.

Certain lizards can detach
their tails. The freed tail
keeps moving on the ground.
This can distract a **predator**
as the lizard runs away.

Grasping and Holding

Some tails are made to grasp and hold objects. Certain monkeys have tails that can hold onto tree branches. They move easily high up in trees.

Seahorses have tails that hold onto ocean plants. This is so the tiny creatures do not float away in the **current**.

More Animal Tails!

Attack
Tail stings and poisons
predators and prey

Communication
Tail slaps against water to
warn others of danger

Finding a Mate
Tail made of beautiful
feathers to attract a mate

Nourishment
Tail stores fat for use
when food is scarce

Pest Control
Tail moves to swat away
flies and other insects

Warmth
Tail wraps around
body for warmth

Glossary

current – a continuous movement of lake or ocean water.

evolved – developed or came into being over time.

grasp – to take hold of.

marine – having to do with the sea.

mate – one of a pair of animals that have young together.

predator – an animal that hunts other animals for food.

prey – an animal that is hunted by other animals for food.

Index

Abdo Kids
ONLINE
FREE! ONLINE MULTIMEDIA RESOURCES

Visit **abdokids.com** to access crafts, games, videos, and more!

Use Abdo Kids code

ADK6288

or scan this QR code!